THE **FUTURE** OF **POWER**

HARNESSING
WAVE AND TIDAL
ENERGY

NANCY DICKMANN

NEW YORK

The Rosen Publishing Group, Inc.
29 East 21st Street, New York, NY 10010

Cataloging-in-Publication Data

Names: Dickmann, Nancy.
Title: Harnessing wave and tidal energy / Nancy Dickmann.
Description: New York : PowerKids Press, 2017. | Series: The future of power | Includes index.
Identifiers: ISBN 9781499432138 (pbk.) | ISBN 9781499432695 (library bound) |
   ISBN 9781508153313 (6 pack)
Subjects: LCSH: Hydroelectric power plants--Juvenile literature. | Water-power--
   Juvenile literature.
Classification: LCC TK1081.D54 2017 | DDC 621.31'2134--dc23

For Brown Bear Books Ltd:
Editor: Tim Harris
Editorial Director: Lindsey Lowe
Children's Publisher: Anne O'Daly
Design Manager: Keith Davis
Picture Manager: Sophie Mortimer

Picture Credits: t=top, c=center, b=bottom, l=left, r=right. Interior: 123rf: 22t, 24; Alamy: Frank Irwin 21t, Peter Jordan 13t, Michael Roper 5; Protean Wave Energy Ltd: Tidal Energy Today 7t; Shutterstock: Marcel Clemens 9b, Leah-Anne Thompson 9t, Daniel Towia 22b; Thinkstock: Digital Vision 7b, istockphoto 19, 21b; Toshiba Japan: Sciencepost.fr 29b; UNC Office of Arts and Science Information Services: 27; US Department of Energy: Water Program/Wave Energy Prize 17b; Wikipedia: Flore Allemandou 11, AW-Energy Oy 29t, Carnegie Wave Energy Limited 17t, P123 15.

Manufactured in the United States of America
CPSIA Compliance Information: Batch #BW17PK: For Further Information contact Rosen Publishing, New York, New York at 1-800-237-9932

CONTENTS

WAVE AND TIDAL POWER

Our modern world depends on energy. From fueling our vehicles to powering our appliances, we use vast amounts of energy every day. A lot of it comes from burning fuels, such as oil, coal, or natural gas. These fuels can be burned directly in vehicles and heating systems, or they can be burned in power stations to generate electricity.

ENERGY FROM MOVEMENT

Any object in motion has a type of energy called kinetic energy. We can convert different forms of kinetic energy into electrical energy. For example, in a power station, burning oil, coal, or natural gas creates heat. The heat is used to turn water into steam, and the steam spins a machine called a turbine, giving it kinetic energy. This kinetic energy is turned into electricity, which is sent through wires to homes and factories.

Scientists and engineers are working on ways to turn other types of kinetic energy, such as wind energy, into electrical energy. The waters of Earth's rivers and oceans have a huge amount of kinetic energy. Harnessing the power of the waves and the tides may help us meet our future energy needs.

ATLANTIS IS THE WORLD'S BIGGEST TIDAL TURBINE. LOCATED IN SCOTLAND, IT CONVERTS KINETIC ENERGY FROM TIDAL CURRENTS INTO ELECTRICITY.

5

OCEANS

Oceans cover more than 70 percent of Earth's surface, and the water in them is constantly on the move. It flows in currents, either near the surface or in the depths, and it also travels as waves. Most waves are formed by the wind blowing over the surface of the ocean. As it blows, the wind's energy is transferred to the water. It pushes the water into swells.

WAVE ENERGY

Out at sea, an average-sized wave is about 10 feet (3 m) high, although during a storm it is common to see waves of 30 feet (9 m) or more. The amount of water in a wave is huge, and it carries a lot of energy. When you think about how vast the oceans are, and how many waves move across their surface, you can easily see why scientists want to harness their power.

The problem with waves is that they occur in oceans. They can't be transported to a power station, like coal and oil can. Instead, engineers have designed different machines that can be installed out at sea. These machines, called wave energy converters (WECs), take the power of the waves' movement and turn it into electrical energy.

WAVE ENERGY CONVERTER

One kind of WEC has a buoy that moves up and down with the action of the waves. The movement creates compressed air that can then be converted into electrical power.

TIDAL ENERGY

Tides are a form of wave that cause the sea to rise and fall along the shore, all over the world. But unlike ocean waves, they are caused by gravity. All objects—including Earth, the Moon, and the Sun—exert a force called gravity. The more massive the object, the bigger the force. Earth's gravity keeps us from flying off into space. The Moon is much smaller, so its gravity is weaker, but it is still strong enough to have an effect on Earth's oceans.

BAY OF FUNDY

The difference between high tide and low tide is called the tidal range. Places with a large tidal range can be good for producing tidal energy. The biggest tidal range is at the Bay of Fundy in Canada.

As the Moon travels around Earth, its gravity pulls the water of the oceans so they bulge out slightly. On the side of the Earth facing the Moon, the sea level rises in a high tide. The opposite side of Earth has a high tide at the same time. Between the two high tides, there is a low tide. As the Moon moves around Earth, so does the bulge. In most places there are two high tides and two low tides each day.

HIGH AND LOW

As it orbits Earth, the Moon's gravity pulls the waters of the oceans, creating the tides. The sea level at high tide is up to 54 feet (16.3 m) higher than at low tide. The seabed that is exposed at low tide (above) is called the intertidal zone.

9

HOW DOES IT WORK?

Using the energy of the tides to power machinery is not a new idea. In fact, tide mills have existed in Europe for hundreds of years. A dam or wall was built to hold in the water when the tide was high. When the tide went out, the water was funneled through a narrow channel, or sluice, where it turned a waterwheel. The waterwheel could then turn various types of machinery, often millstones for grinding grain into flour.

Tide mills were common along the Atlantic coast of colonial America, but by the 20th century they were no longer very useful—more efficient ways to power machinery had been discovered. However, some engineers began to wonder if the tides could be put to good use generating electricity.

TIDAL BARRAGE

In the 1930s, the government of President Franklin D. Roosevelt invested money in research into tidal energy, but no plants were ever built. The first tidal power station was built in northern France, on the estuary of the Rance River. It opened in 1966 and for decades it had the highest output of any tidal power station in the world.

RIVER AND TIDE MILLS

A river mill works all the time the river is flowing. The wheel of a tide mill turns only when the tide is rising or falling.

The power plant on the Rance River is a type of installation called a tidal barrage. A low dam, or barrage, is built across a bay or river estuary. The barrage allows water in at high tide, and at low tide it lets the water out through sluice gates. The sluice gates have turbines that spin around as the water flows out. The spinning motion generates electricity.

TIDAL LAGOON

Another type of installation is a tidal lagoon, which is similar to a tidal barrage. However, in a tidal lagoon the area of water is only partly enclosed, either by natural barriers or artificial walls. Turbines in the barriers generate electricity as the lagoon fills and empties. Tidal lagoons can be built from natural materials along the existing coastline.

Another technology is called a tidal stream generator, and it is a bit like an underwater wind turbine. These turbines are installed below the surface in a channel where the tide flows quickly. They turn slowly as the water rushes past.

WATER FLOWING IN A RIVER CAN BE HARNESSED TO GENERATE ELECTRICITY.

TIDAL STREAM GENERATOR

A tidal stream generator has underwater blades that turn turbines when a current flows past them.

13

A PELAMIS WAVE ENERGY CONVERTER HAS SEVERAL CONNECTED SECTIONS. THESE BEND AS WAVES PASS. THE MOTION GENERATES ELECTRICITY.

14

The use of wave energy is a newer idea. Engineers began to investigate ways of harnessing the power of waves in the 19th century. Then, in 1910, a French engineer invented a device that could provide light and power for his house. The machine was called an oscillating water column, or OWC. It consisted of a vertical chamber drilled into a cliff. When waves made the water level in the chamber rise, it pushed out the air at the top of the column. The air was forced out through a turbine, which spun to generate electricity.

There are many other methods of generating electricity from waves. Depending on the type of device, the hardware can be installed on the shore, near the shore, or out at sea. Some devices float on the surface, and others are hidden beneath the waves. Engineers are working on designing new technologies, as well as making the existing ones more efficient.

"WHISTLING BUOYS"

The first OWC machines—called "whistling buoys"—were off the east coast of the United States. Wave action forced air out of a hole in the top of the buoy, making a whistle. This warned sailors that the coast was nearby.

15

An oscillating wave surge converter is used in shallow water. It has a flap anchored to the seabed. Connected to the flap is a paddle that moves back and forth with the horizontal movement of the water. In some devices the paddle reaches above the surface, and in others it is completely submerged.

POINT ABSORBERS

A point absorber is a machine that has two main parts. The top part floats near the surface. It is connected to a bottom part that can either float beneath it or be attached to the seabed. The top part rises and falls as swells move past it. This up-and-down motion relative to the fixed base is converted into electrical power.

A Ceto device is a type of point absorber. It is installed completely beneath the surface, out of sight. It consists of a buoy tethered to a hydraulic pump on the seabed. When the buoy moves up and down with the waves, the pump forces pressurized water through a pipeline. The pressurized water ends up at a facility on the shore, where it spins a turbine to generate electricity.

AMAZING CETO

Ceto devices are named for the mythological Greek sea goddess, Ceto. Some of the electricity they produce from the motion of waves is used to convert salty ocean water into drinkable freshwater.

HIDDEN FROM VIEW

Several Ceto pods are tethered to the seabed off the coast of Australia. They are completely submerged. As the pods move up and down with the waves, they generate electricity. This is wired to the shore.

THIS WAVE ENERGY CONVERTER IS BEING LOWERED INTO THE OCEAN.

17

GOOD AND BAD

Wave and tidal power are just two of the ways of producing energy that are currently being developed. Governments and corporations are interested in investing in wave and tidal power because these two types of energy are renewable. This means that they are based on things that will never run out or be used up.

The world's supply of fuels such as oil is limited, and once we have extracted it all, there won't be any more. At the moment, we depend heavily on oil and other non-renewable fuels such as coal and natural gas. They are used in power stations, and provide fuel for airplanes, cars, trains, and heating systems. But experts believe that it is only a matter of time before oil and gas start to run out.

RENEWABLES

Unlike oil, the energy of the oceans will never run out. It is a renewable form of energy. There will always be waves and tides, containing a vast amount of energy. Using their energy to meet our needs is a better option in the long run. However, there is a long way to go before these technologies are able to replace oil, coal, and gas.

WAVES WILL NEVER RUN OUT.
THAT MAKES WAVES A GOOD
SOURCE OF RENEWABLE POWER.

19

Another advantage of wave and tidal power is that compared to other technologies, they are fairly "clean." This means they do not cause much pollution or damage to the environment. More importantly, they do not lead to the emission of carbon dioxide.

When oil, coal, and gas are burned, they release a gas called carbon dioxide. Relatively small amounts of carbon dioxide are already present in the atmosphere—in fact, we breathe it out all the time! But when there is too much carbon dioxide in the atmosphere, it can trap the Sun's heat, instead of allowing it to escape into space. It acts in a similar way to the panes of glass in a greenhouse, so this is usually called the "greenhouse effect."

GREENHOUSE EFFECT

The greenhouse effect is causing a rise in Earth's average temperature, which could lead to huge changes in the climate. Governments are looking for new ways to generate energy that don't contribute to the greenhouse effect. Once they are running, these technologies do not create carbon emissions or other pollution.

SEA LEVEL RISE
Rising global temperatures caused by the greenhouse effect will melt massive amounts of ice in the Antarctic and Arctic. This will increase the sea level and cause flooding in some coastal areas.

CLEAN ENERGY

This tidal turbine is being prepared for installation on the seabed near Scotland. It will produce "clean" energy, without the dirty smoke of a coal-burning power station (below).

WAVE ENERGY CONVERTERS HAVE TO BE LOCATED WITH CARE TO AVOID DISRUPTING THE ROUTES USED BY SHIPS.

HABITAT DISTURBANCE

One major disadvantage of tidal barrages is that they may disrupt intertidal zones, on which many animals depend for their food.

Although wave energy is clean and renewable, it does have disadvantages. One is that it can only be used in locations that are near the ocean. Cities near the coast have to put wave energy installations well away from beaches and busy shipping lanes.

DOLPHINS AND WHALES

Dolphins and whales have a very good sense of hearing. They are sensitive to loud sounds. Scientists worry that the noise of building a wave farm may frighten these animals away.

UNDERWATER NOISE

Wave energy can also cause problems for ocean life. When the machines are installed, they often disturb the seabed. Animals such as crabs and starfish may find their habitats disturbed or even destroyed. When they are operating, wave machines create noise under the water. Creatures that use sound to communicate, such as whales and dolphins, will keep well away.

One of the biggest problems is cost. The technology is still very new and needs more investment. Electricity produced by wave power is still more expensive than that produced by burning coal or natural gas.

Like wave power, tidal energy has the advantage of being clean, renewable, and abundant, but it also has its own problems. Compared to waves, tides are more constant and easier to predict. However, a tidal power station can only generate power during tidal surges, or about 10 hours a day. At other times, different types of power must be used.

Wave power is limited to locations near the coast, and tidal power is even more limited. There are not that many places on Earth where the difference between high and low tide is big enough to make tidal power efficient.

Tidal power stations are expensive to build, although they are fairly cheap to run once they're in place. But there is an environmental cost: river estuaries are important ecosystems, and building a barrage across one can harm the plants and animals that live there.

BIGGEST WAVE FARM

Work on the world's biggest wave farm, in Scotland, will start in 2017. When complete, this facility will provide electricity for 30,000 homes.

TIDAL ENERGY CANNOT BE GENERATED AT THOSE TIMES OF THE DAY WHEN THE WATER IS STILL.

25

THE FUTURE

Wave and tidal power make up only a small fraction of the total power that we use. In the future they will probably become more important. However, for that to happen the technology must become cheaper and more efficient. Engineers are working on new designs that will be able to compete with other types of energy.

One new technology is the Azura device, a type of point absorber. It can generate electricity by moving up and down with the waves, and also when it moves horizontally with the swells.

Engineers in Canada have developed a floating tidal power plant. A specially built barge has turbines within it that spin with the tides to generate electricity. This system has less of an impact on coastal ecosystems than a tidal barrage does. It can also operate in fairly shallow water.

WAVE POTENTIAL

Scientists estimate that wave power could eventually provide about 10 percent of the world's energy needs.

THIS AZURA WAVE MACHINE IS BEING TESTED IN HAWAII. IT WILL BE USED TO SUPPLY ENERGY TO THE ISLANDS' ELECTRICITY GRID.

27

Different shapes of seabed-mounted tidal turbines are also being tested. Some look like wind turbines, and others are shaped more like screws. There is even one called a "tidal kite," that is tethered to the seabed and "flies" in the tidal stream. Wave and tidal power have the potential to provide huge amounts of energy, but it will take time. The world's first wave farm opened in Portugal in 2008 but soon closed due to financial difficulties. Although many projects are in development, there are only a handful of commercial wave power installations.

Tidal power is more established, but only in a few countries, such as France, South Korea, Canada, and China. Aside from the Rance and Sihwa Lake, most tidal power stations generate only a few megawatts of electricity. One megawatt is enough to power a few hundred homes.

INVESTMENT

If governments and businesses invest money to improve the technology, it will become cheaper to generate wave and tidal power. These power installations will become more common along the world's coasts.

TIDAL POTENTIAL
Scientists estimate that if we built tidal barrages in all the suitable locations, it could generate up to 7 percent of the world's electricity production.

WAVEROLLER

The WaveRoller is one of the most modern oscillating wave surge converters. It was installed off Portugal in 2009. The device has a plate anchored to the seabed. The motion of waves moves the plate, driving a piston pump and making electricity.

IN THE FUTURE LARGE UNDERWATER TURBINE FARMS MAY BE BUILT. THEY WILL GENERATE "CLEAN" ENERGY FROM TIDAL CURRENTS.

GLOSSARY

buoy: A floating object that is anchored to the seabed.

compressed air: Air that has been squeezed into a small space.

current: The movement of water beneath the surface of the ocean.

ecosystems: A community of plants and animals that interact with each other and their environment.

emissions: The discharge of gases and particles into the atmosphere.

estuary: The mouth of a large river, where the freshwater of the river meets the ocean tides.

generator: A device that turns mechanical energy into electricity.

gravity: The force that attracts a physical object to the center of the Earth or toward another physical body with mass.

hydraulic pump: A device that converts mechanical energy into a flow of water or another fluid.

intertidal zone: The seabed that is exposed at low tide.

orbit: The curved path of something around a planet, moon, or star.

piston pump: A cylinder that moves inside a tube to squeeze a liquid or gas and produce motion.

pollution: The release of substances that have harmful or toxic effects into the atmosphere, rivers, or ocean.

tethered: Tied to the seabed.

tide: The rise and fall in sea level. The tidal range is the difference in height between high and low tides.

turbine: A machine with blades attached to a central rotating shaft. Turbines are used to generate electricity.

FURTHER INFORMATION

BOOKS

Challoner, Jack. *Energy* (Eyewitness).
New York: Dorling Kindersley, 2012.

Dickmann, Nancy. *Energy from Water: Hydroelectric, Tidal, and Wave Power.* New York: Crabtree, 2016.

Rusch, Elizabeth. *The Next Wave: The Quest to Harness the Power of the Oceans* (Scientists in the Field). Boston: Houghton Mifflin Harcourt, 2014.

WEBSITES

Due to the changing nature of Internet links, PowerKids Press has developed an online list of websites related to the subject of this book. This site is updated regularly. Please use this link to access the list:

www.powerkidslinks.com/tfop/wave

INDEX